I0518993

Amanda M Renaud

CEO of Magnetic Entrepreneur Inc.

Songs About Sunflowers

Legal Disclaimer

Copyright © 2024 SONGS ABOUT SUNFLOWERS. Amanda M Renaud. All rights reserved worldwide.

No part of this material may be used, reproduced, distributed or transmitted in any form and by any means whatsoever, including without limitation photocopying, recording or other electronic or mechanical methods or by any information storage and retrieval system, without the prior written permission from the author, except for brief excerpts in a review. This book is intended to provide general information only. Neither the author nor publisher provides any legal or other professional advice. If you need professional advice, you should seek advice from the appropriate licensed professional. This book does not provide complete information on the subject matter covered. This book is not intended to address specific requirements, either for an individual or an organization. This book is intended to be used only as a general guide, and not as a sole source of information on the subject matter. While the author has undertaken diligent efforts to ensure accuracy, there is no guarantee of accuracy or of no errors, omissions or typographical errors. Any slights of people or organizations are unintentional. The author and publisher shall have no liability or responsibility to any person or entity and hereby disclaim all liability, including without limitation, liability for consequential damages regarding any claim, loss or damage that may be incurred, or alleged to have been incurred, directly or indirectly, arising out of the information provided in this book.

Copyright © 2024 by Amanda M Renaud.
All rights reserved. No part of this publication may be reproduced or transmitted in any form or by any means, electronic, or mechanical, including photocopying, recording, or by any information storage and retrieval system.

DEDICATION

I would like to dedicate this book to all the courageous survivors who have persevered, taken their pain and tribulations and turned them into beautiful opportunities that have changed their own lives as well as others around them.

Let your sense of conquering adversity always shine through all that you do and become.

Acknowledgements

I would like to acknowledge the founder of Magnetic Entrepreneur, Robert J Moore, and his ongoing support, mentorship, and continued hard work. In addition, I would like to thank Dr. Marianne Padjan for her foreword and exceptional leadership.

I am thankful for the co-authors and their courageous contributions and hard work. We welcome them into the world of writing and wish them much success and continued levels of resilience.

I would also like to acknowledge all the hard-working entrepreneurs, and wonderful authors past and present of the brand Magnetic Entrepreneur Inc. May we all strive to be magnetic and create lasting contributions that impact and change the lives of businesses all over the globe.

May we remember the struggles and difficulties of our lives and continue to support and empower others through our legacies, brands and creations. May we always show kindness and compassion in each industry and strive to be Magnetic Masterminds who change the world.

Amanda M Renaud

TABLE OF CONTENTS

Contents

Contents

FOREWORD

Have you ever held a sunflower in your hand? Its vibrant petals and towering stem radiate beauty and strength. But beyond their physical attributes, sunflowers possess a remarkable endurance that allows them to stand tall and last for an exceptionally long time. In many ways, they serve as a powerful metaphor for the human spirit.

If someone has compared you to a sunflower, it is because they recognize your authentic power. Perhaps you have faced and conquered significant obstacles and adversity in your life. You have shown resilience and the ability to rise above challenges, just like a sunflower emerges from dry soil with the help of nurturing. You are not easily shaken or defeated; you have a core strength that shines through.

This book brings together a carefully selected group of authors who embody the sunflower spirit. Their energy and life experiences serve as a testament to the fact that the presence of roadblocks does not dictate whether or not they will reach their destination. The authors' stories will inspire and motivate you to embrace your own inner sunflower.

Life has a way of throwing curveballs at us when we least expect it. We all face trials and tribulations along our journey. Yet, the authors within these pages show you that you have the power to overcome any challenge and emerge victorious. They remind you that you, too, can be a sunflower in life and come out on top.

In a field of daylilies, be a sunflower !! Embrace your individuality and let your authentic power shine. By being true to yourself and embracing your unique qualities, you will not only inspire yourself but also those around you.

This book serves as an invitation to rise above adversity and awaken your inner sunflower. It urges you to sing your song so that others can sing along with you. Let your voice be heard, share your experiences, and motivate others to embrace their own sunflower spirit.

Throughout this book, the writing will be infused with a motivational tone. Each author's story, wisdom, and guidance will provide you with the tools and inspiration to tap into your authentic power. So, prepare yourself to embark on a transformative journey as you discover how to embrace your inner sunflower and embody your true potential.

It is time to blossom, to stand tall, and to become the sunflower you were destined to be. Let the stories shared within this book serve as a guiding light, illuminating the path to your own greatness. Your journey starts now.

Dr. Marianne Padjan
Spiritualtouch11@gmail.com

INTRODUCTION

Sunflowers are more than just late fall flowers. They are a sacred symbol that signifies resilience and growth despite upheaval, and the struggles of their environment. They grow tall and capture the eyes of everyone in their path. Sunflowers have an innate ability to adapt to their environment. Despite the harsh climate and weather they face, they remain defiant and create hundreds of little seeds that flourish and those seeds also bloom.

Sunflowers radiate bright and beautiful colours that attract pollinators. These pollinators cherish the sunflower and help it to grow. The sunflower then blooms and its beauty cannot be forgotten. Like the sunflower, there are many souls who face harsh life conditions and suffer immensely throughout their lives. In this life, there will be struggles and pain, and there will be sacrifice and events that will bring us to our knees.

However, like the sunflower, these souls adapt, and they bloom no matter what affliction they suffer. These individuals plant seeds of hope and remind us that positive change lies ahead. These individuals, known as sunflowers, often sing songs of success and demonstrate strength and they possess grit and inspire us to reach for the light through darkness.

They have demonstrated an extraordinary level of healing, growth and courage to share their stories. In this novel, you will find their stories and how they bloomed in order to plant seeds for others in their fields and change the world around them.

As you read their stories, you will come to find that the sunflower captures the audience of all who embrace its beauty and is a remarkable measurement of strength, resilience, and growth. The soul of a sunflower will forever be the wildflower that can turn the pain and struggle of our unique life experiences into journeys worthy of capturing and admiring.

Enclosed are their stories that we refer to as songs because they will be remembered and sung for generations to come. Let us remember, in life, we can overcome anything and despite the hardships of the seasons of life, we must always remember how the sunflower is a reminder that all beautiful things eventually bloom.

Amanda M Renaud

Chapter 1

A SONG OF A SUNFLOWER

Amanda M Renaud

When I think of sunflowers, a personal passion of mine, I always light up. They are one of my favourite flowers and the inspiration behind creating this book. This book collaboration's purpose was in hope of sharing, like the sunflower, a radiant side of resilience that could inspire, captivate, and bring forth the comparative beauty of the sunflower to the expression of human experiences.

Many who know of me, my writings, and stories, know pieces of my story, which are not-so-pleasant experiences that I have conquered. In my chapter, I will be sharing my story of resilience. It all started when I was in college; it was my final year. I wasn't in college like most young people. I was a bit older and had more responsibilities as I was also a mom to a young boy and recovering from a life-altering motor vehicle accident.

The results of this accident permeated every aspect of my life, so it required a lot of time and commitment to recover. I had a commitment to growth and getting better. I had a commitment to another human life and my education. It was a very difficult and challenging time of life for me.

During that time period, I was also going through a long-term relationship breakup and the usual life stressors. It required full-time focus, and with litigation in the background from a car accident and medical issues, my plate was very full. Most people at that time of life were a lot younger and just not at the same stage

or really dealing with such comprehensive issues, so it was often hard for me to feel like I truly fit in anywhere I went.

Regardless, I did end up making some good friends, but was met with some harsh lessons when it came to interpersonal relationships. The relationship had ended in December of the previous year on my birthday, coming home to a vague letter, an empty home and really a ton of questions and disappointment.

Just a few months later, I would get a call that would change my life and that of my family. That particular day, I received a call from the local police station, a young officer asking me if I was alone and if I could get to my mom's house. Ironically, my therapist was also on his way for our ten a.m. session. I let the police know I would be heading there shortly. The police were very tight-lipped and wouldn't respond to my probing questions if everything was alright and what this was about.

When my therapist called, moments after, I explained about the troubling call I had received. At this point, I had a feeling and an overwhelming suspicion. I let my therapist know and he offered to drive me over to my mom's down the road. I remember the drive because of the conversation that took place. He also, would remember it and come to the conclusion that I had strong intuition and was a very articulate young lady. My therapist was one of my favourite people, a positive and happy elderly man, brilliant and always well-dressed. He was someone who changed my life and made an immense difference and positive impact on me. I had a sense of humour and was rather blunt after my accident and we had many laughs.

During that drive to my mom's, he knew right away, as did I, that something serious was happening. When I got in the car, he handed me a coffee and I buckled my belt and looked up and he said, "Are you okay?" I told him I was fine but knew he could visibly see my anxious discomfort and worry. I felt this overwhelming urge and the words just came out. I looked up and straight ahead. I said to him, "I think she's dead, I think it's my sister." I looked over at his face and he wasn't shocked or surprised.

As we approached the front of my mother's home, there were four police cars in their parking lot. I had said this out loud and now his response was him asking if I wanted him to come upstairs with me or how he could best support me in that moment. I felt impending doom and just mentioned that I would be okay and that I would give him an update later. We said our goodbyes and as I exited the vehicle, I had this feeling that was just over the top — likely adrenaline and anxiety.

As I opened the first screen door to get to the apartment door, I could already hear voices and crying. I walked up the stairs to see many officers and many immediate family members with faces drowned in tears. I don't recall all the details, but I do recall my mom and the officers telling me the news and I was shocked that my intuition was so accurate.

I didn't say much but walked to the backdoor, took my sandals off and lay in the grass. With the grass between my fingertips, my body lay against the cold soil, rock, and grass. I remember the tears streaming down my face in an endless flow, and screams of pain could be heard throughout the quiet neighbourhood in our small town.

Our home was filled with officers and family. This was something that would change my life. You see, just one call is all it takes, and a new reality is formed. A reality that you had wished was not true. The screams and cries of my mother and siblings are sounds I will never forget. Sounds that haunt my mind. And this would not be the last time I would hear a mother scream for a child she has lost. It is a sound that your mind will never erase, and to think of those screams brings tears to your soul.

Often, we do not think that losing someone is a potential threat in our day-to-day lives, but it is. That is why we must always love and show kindness. I am forever a sunflower because of my human experiences. I had to find strength during loss that I didn't know I had.

When I envision a sunflower, I think of how hardy, beautiful, and strong a sunflower must be. The harsh environment a sunflower faces in order to grow tall and spread its beauty like wildfire must be endured. A sunflower is always reaching for the light and exists in such a way that it captures the eyes of every living creature that passes.

I like to think of myself as a sunflower. Throughout my life, I have faced loss after loss, goodbye after goodbye, and so that leaves a certain kind of emptiness and a feeling of somberness. It can fill your soul with songs of sorrow, and written below is mine. That day changed my life, and somehow, that morning, I knew the years that would follow would be difficult for myself and my family.

I would lose much of myself and battle my reality. During the first few months, I lay in my bed most of the time. When I did go out, it was dangerous. I had no fear anymore. Disassociated from

the world around me, I was cold and angry most of the time. I not only lost my sister but my first real love.

This trauma would change me as a person, and it would destroy everything I believed about love and family. I was already grieving about my health loss from a car accident and now grieving for people I truly valued and loved. I engaged in risky behaviour for over a year. It was something I'd later regret and feel shame about.

I was searching for ways to fill the empty void and feel something. The numbness that I embraced was a self-sabotaging method. I was still achieving and going to school, but there were so many friends and people around me who treated me poorly, and I will never forget that type of betrayal.

Sometimes people think they're helping, but well some of them were just cruel. It taught me very quickly that I was going to have to make significant changes and fast. I began working out for hours and hours a day and quit drinking. I became obsessed with running on my treadmill. It made me feel alive. I would do this several times a day. I began reading more and writing a lot more. I changed my diet and made a decision. I was going to get out of bed.

Several professionals had expressed to me that my organs were shutting down, and if I didn't change my lifestyle, I would die. After that news, I was devastated, and of course, the conversation came to be about having a hysterectomy. It was believed that because of my accident, I could not have any more children. My body simply couldn't physically handle that.

All of this news forced me to really analyze what I was grieving and to separate each circumstance and face it head-on.

There wasn't much I could change other than myself. I began hiking, doing yoga, physio, and engaging in a strict routine. I started rebuilding who I was.

Although I remained positive and focused my time on my studies and working with youth, I was struggling immensely inside. There were times I couldn't even hear my sister's name or look at her picture without breaking down. Time progressed, and I was soon able to articulate my feelings. What came out was an overwhelming feeling of guilt. I felt guilt because days prior to my sister's passing, we had a huge fight over a dress and concert. I chalked it up to a silly fight. I didn't ever think she would take her own life or that she was suffering.

A part of me felt like I could have done more and should have known, and that was the hardest reality for me to face. I questioned if that fight had gone differently, would she still be here? To this day, I hate arguing with anyone or leaving things unsettled. I soon came to realize that I had no control over the way life happened to me. Later, I would adopt the mantra that "Life happened for me, not to me." It's something that still brings much emotion and I dread having to tell this story to anyone in person because of the myths around suicide and what people believe about it.

Society has many misconceptions regarding suicide and academically, they can all be dismissed by facts. In recent years, things have gotten much better, but it is a piece of dark family history that haunts and affects the family unit for many generations. My sister's eldest daughter lives with us and has been a great addition to our family unit.

Over recent years, we have healed and grown as a family for the most part and gotten closer. After conquering many life events and traumas, I found the strength to adapt to life and build a healthier lifestyle. There certainly were many moments that were tough but having a strong support system and choosing healthier life options did make a difference.

To this day I rarely drink and have learned how to take care of my body, mind and soul. I ended up finishing school, writing a few books that became international best sellers and recently bought a publishing company from my long-term coach and publisher. Robert has been a wonderful support who really inspired me to write and keep on the path I was pursuing my goals.

I also learned how to be strong and push through the worst storms in order to thrive again. Of course, I made mistakes along my path, but I helped some, inspired some and learned life lessons that have influenced me to be a better person. I think in life there are so many things that happen to us, and at the time, we often don't understand that they will be moments of significant paradigm shifts in our character that shape the way our future will look.

You have to really want something bad enough in life to go after it and you have to have the courage to survive. When you have to survive loss after loss, it can be exhausting, and it becomes harder to make true living come back. I had to fight a lot of inner toxic traits and work much harder at things than the average person because of my injuries, and I also learned to see the world in a different light.

I often found refuge in my reading, writing, and gardening. I grew a genuine adoration for sunflowers because of their grit and beauty. I often saw more than just a sunflower when I would be out in the garden which inspired this book series, and I sought after unique individuals who had conquered life's storms and had displayed admirable strength in life and had the courage to speak up in hopes of showing others that no matter your circumstance or environment, you can still flourish and become anything you want.

When I connect with others, I hear their stories and continue to be inspired. I've always admired the sunflower the most of all the beautiful plants I have grown. When I would be in my garden and look at everything I had created, the sunflower was like looking into a mirror. I would inspect my garden daily and see how the wind and weather would damage my plants over the summer but never the sunflower.

They may have wilted a little bit, but they always rose and reached for the sky. There is so much over just one decade that has challenged me and caused me to grow even stronger. Maybe during some of the storms I faced, it took time to regain my strength again, but I always have come back stronger and more focused. When I used to tell people that I was going to be an author and write books, they often laughed and never believed in me. That was one of my biggest motivators to do so and excel at it.

Many would often try to discourage me from engaging in life experiences because they seemed too big to them, but for me, I will always challenge myself and continue to share my story because surviving has become my expertise. I say this because, through all the loss and elemental forces of life, I always followed what I

wanted and did my best to prove to my children and myself that you can overcome anything and turn something negative and destructive into something beautiful.

For most of the last decade, I have been assessed and tested in the medical community. It was examination after examination, appointment after appointment. Seeing on paper the type of damage that had been done and reading the reports was a huge motivator for me. I never wanted to just be Amanda who almost died in a car accident. I knew that couldn't be my story and my end. I also gone through grief, abandonment, health issues and mental illness in just one year. That year was a milestone, a formidable milestone that I still am so thankful to have safely passed.

Amanda M Renaud

Amanda is a 36-year-old professional from a small town in Canada, called Waubaushene, where she lives in a rural community with her three sons and family. Amanda has a diploma in child and youth treatment and is a certified Transformational Life Coach and the CEO of Magnetic Entrepreneur Inc.

Former Founder, Robert J Moore, a bestselling author, sold the business to Amanda in September 2023. Robert has been featured in Forbes and has been a big part of Amanda's journey through entrepreneurship and, of course, a huge inspiration.

Amanda is also an international Bestselling Author and has been an author with Magnetic Entrepreneur herself. She really

valued her experience being an author which fueled her to bigger goals.

Amanda hopes to continue the success and achievements Magnetic Entrepreneur has had on a global level, winning a Global recognition award in 2023 and a Guinness World Record in 2020.

Amanda is passionate about nature, family, self-development, and leadership. She is a survivor of a life-changing car accident in 2010 that had a profound impact on her; she has worked hard to change her life and build a brighter future.

She is passionate about helping others and making a positive impact in the writing community, committed to her coaching services and has over 20 years of leadership experience.

To contact Amanda:

(705) 427-2730

Magneticpublishing2023@gmail.com

www.magnetic-entrepreneur.com

Chapter 2

EXPERIENCE THE LIGHT OF DIVINITY

Mandy E. Robinson

Absolutely captivating!! A vast expanse of arrayed, riveting yellow, intertwining leaves surrounding palettes of black hues hovering upwards on the crest of a light breeze. Absolutely captivating!! Have you ever looked into the face of a sunflower? I mean REALLY looked deeply into the makeup of the face of a sunflower? Have you dared to dance to the song of a host of sunflowers?

When I imagine sunflowers, I'm inspired to write poetic renditions of how they make me feel, how they permeate my spirit with their faces smiling brilliantly back at me in the warm, sun-lit cascading rays of vibrant dynamic energy. Even when cloud cover makes it appear as if their light will fade for a short while, they staunchly hold their ground in the knowledge that their radiant light will shine once more through the power from the life-giving luminary above. The great Sun God, an extension of the universal creator of all life referred to in an ancient script as, *"an abundance of dynamic energy."*

How can you comprehend the depth of His wisdom in creation? You cannot because He is the Alpha and the Omega, the one without beginning or end. Way beyond the comprehension of mere mortals. As the ancient Biblical writer also pens, *"His thoughts are higher than our thoughts, and His ways higher than our ways!"*

The sun came warmly through my window caressing my soul just like it does for each sunflower, boding well for the international speaker's poetry conference that I was honoured to take part in on that fateful day soon to reveal itself. I was well prepared to share my poetic wisdom on the theme of coming from a place of love in all that we think, say, and do.

The conference had begun approximately one-half hour just before I was alerted to the sound of alarming pounding on my door, urgent, compelling, and relentless. I excused myself from the platform to answer the door. As I opened the door the smell of smoke came pouring into my kitchen.

I was in complete dismay to see a young lady distraught and yelling, "There's a fire, there's a fire, I can't make her hear me next door!" she cried out. I put my head out of the door, turning to the left from whence the smoke came, and saw the second house from the end of our row of townhouses on fire as smoke billowed out of it.

My home is the fourth house from the end. At first, it was dense grey-coloured smoke, which very quickly turned to an ugly dense black toxic smoke, yes, the kind of smoke that can kill a life very rapidly! It was leaping into the atmosphere and spreading in all directions. People later commented that they could smell the smoke that day from 4 km away!

My instinct went into high gear as I looked around quickly for something hard to put in my hand that I might need as blunt force to smash a door window. It was all happening at an accelerated speed; there was no time to think, only act. My next-door neighbour has a young child with cystic fibrosis and smoke inhalation would be lethal to their survival.

I grabbed my keys and turned to their back door where a

security camera was installed, I yelled and yelled and kept yelling into the camera, whilst pounding on my neighbour's door, "Get out!! Get out!! There's a fire!! Get out!!"

I know that they liked to sleep in on weekends, and wasn't sure if they could hear me. The smoke was beginning to infiltrate my breathing and overcome me, I had to back away, falling down the steps of the deck onto the grass.

There was pandemonium in every direction as people screamed and yelled get away from the houses! Get as far away from the houses as you can! I recall. I remember running to the other end of the row to pound on other neighbours' doors to get out. A voice was screaming above the noise, "Switch the hydro off!! Then I found myself on a step further away, looking at the flames catapulting as they breached every crevice they could find, growing higher and higher relishing their freedom!

The ferocity of the lurching flames seemed inescapable! You could almost hear them speak over and around you, magnetizing you into their vortex of destruction. They had a sadistic air about their approach.

Since when was an inferno ever a safe haven of desire? The heat, if you can imagine, was unbearable forcing you to get as far away as possible and as quickly as possible.

My lungs were choking as I sat there coughing and trying to breathe oxygen from anywhere possible, whilst holding a tea towel over my mouth. I was now crying and shaking from the shock at what had unfolded in only eight and a half minutes! So, I began to

try to walk away, but quickly found myself subdued to crawling away.

I could feel the intense heat on my back; debris was flying in every direction as the hydro lines exploded along the row of houses. Some hit my back as I crawled away. The explosions were like missiles raining down on the complex. The scene resembled the depictions of Armageddon.

I did look back and actually saw my neighbour at the door in a white house coat. "Thank you," I said looking up. The song of the sunflower pointing its face to the sky where the warmth and light of love were, had me fervently singing in my soul and I found a serene peace transcending the chaos, to put me in Divine alignment. It was so surreal to experience this interlude at this moment in time.

I made it to the end of the complex and collapsed choking to breathe. I remember two police officers coming and picking me up and taking me to an ambulance, where it was soon discovered that my heart had gone into Atrial fibrillation. The trauma was real, the shock was stunning every fibre of my being as I fought to breathe. Oxygen soon helped as I rode to the hospital.

Once there, I lay thinking, that the only things I had to my name at that point were the smoky putrid-smelling clothes on my back and the keys in my hand. Tears began to fall as I pondered, "Did anyone make it out alive? Is my home still standing? I have no way of knowing." Closing my eyes to enable sleep and waking to find it was all just a nightmare would be a welcoming reprieve at best.

Alas, sleep evaded me. I was left on oxygen, my heart was stabilized over the next few hours and I was told they would keep me in overnight to monitor me. However, at the change of shift for

personnel, I was informed that they weren't going to keep me as I had been stabilized satisfactorily and could go home. "But I don't know if

I have a home to go to, there was a fire," I cried.

Over the course of the next few hours, I would learn that all pets had perished. I would find myself homeless, sitting in my car by the lake before walking to the shoreline to ponder and meditate and ask Source what direction I must take. At this point, I was directed to go to a local hotel that would kindly put me up until Monday when the Insurance Company could be reached. Yes, my insurance company was closed on weekends! You might want to take a look at and review your own policies.

So, depleted of all drive, motivation and energy, smelling of smoke, in shock and traumatized, I found myself in front of staff who had nothing but kindness and understanding of what I needed to find some solace amidst the tragedy. Nothing was too much trouble for any one of them. I felt some sense of relief and deep gratitude that I would not be spending two nights in my car!

Little did I know that a single room in this hotel would become my home for ten weeks! Also, I would have great difficulty attaining more than two to three hours per night of sleep for the whole duration, or I would have ongoing nightmares that had me waking into what I believed was my reality.

I didn't know that post-traumatic stress disorder would slowly seep in as I tried to navigate this strange way of living that had been brought upon me through no fault of my own. My whole world, my whole life would be turned inside out and upside down leaving me feeling lost, vulnerable, numb at times, and emotional, at others.

I felt as if I fit in nowhere, belonged nowhere, I just was … period. Whilst I often enunciated loud and clear that I was doing this

all on my own, without support, I knew that even the heavy-weighted head of the sunflower that seemed too heavy for its stem to bear; stood elegantly, proud, glowing with Divine sunlight strengthening its stem with the greatest of ease. I too would have a purpose for being there in that hotel for all that time. All I had to do was turn my face to the sun's rays and all would be made clear, the warmth and light would ignite my spirit to stand strong and supported to do what I love to do best, inspire others to find their own light and shine too.

I'd spend a lot of time in the restaurant for most of my meals where I would come to know the names of most of the service staff who would eagerly stop to talk, and our conversations would organically come to be. From inspiring a young teacher with ADHD to say that I was the first person who had ever really understood her, and had great empathy and compassion, that she felt she should pay me $20,000!; to a greeter who apologized if it appeared to me that he was eavesdropping on my conversations with others. "You have so much wisdom and I want to learn as much from you as I can." To another time, "I need inspiring — tell me something inspiring!" To "How's our resident guru of great wisdom today?"

Hotel reception staff would say they absolutely loved having me stay there and I loved greeting them every morning! Maid service attendants would echo the same, "We all love you." I would go and search for the person who had made my room up in an extra special way to say thank you, they would smile and say it's a pleasure to see you smile, that's why we did it, because of your beautiful heart.

This sunflower was singing her inspiration wherever she went with simple, random acts of kindness that came organically from my

heart. The owners even commented that I had become part of the family and we enjoyed many a productive and fun conversation over time. Everywhere I went in that hotel, I smiled, held my head up like the sunflower. I openly welcomed everyone and received joyous responses. My heart shone with gratitude as I moved around.

Looking back, I now know that I was placed there, at that time to be an inspiration and encouragement to many. There is indeed more happiness in giving than in receiving as the greatest man who ever lived advocated. As the phoenix rose from the ashes, this sunflower sang her heart out, held her head above and continues to rise from the ashes of devastation in the aftermath.

The greatest gift to me in all of this?

One day I found myself at the house grabbing a few things I knew I needed. The back door was open as I couldn't breathe easily in the toxic environment. The next-door neighbour was standing on the deck speaking with another family of the four affected by the fire. I could hear their words clearly. "Honestly? Mandy saved our lives! I was in the shower! If I hadn't paid attention to Mandy's insistent banging on the door and her assertive voice, we wouldn't be here today!" I heard my neighbour say this with gratitude in her voice. Her words fell like nectar upon my soul, and I wept with joy.

Everything I do, I do from a place of love without any expectations. I had not looked for and neither did I need thanks for helping them, but this validation and appreciation was meant for me to receive, and receive it I did, with humble, silent gratitude. I felt so blessed to be alive in that moment.

The sunflower goes through many stages of growth before it can shine its glory before the world. Yet it sings its song excitedly along its journey to the sun's rays. It is relentless in its purpose,

quitting is not even an option, it is born to shine!

Can you be like the sunflower? I would have to adamantly say

YES you can!

I would like you to think of the word impermanence, which brings our minds to awareness; awareness that nothing, not even time, ever stays the same as life evolves, ever-changing, moment by moment. This perspective can help you to never give up.

Being mindful helps you to change the negative, reactive thoughts to any dilemma you might face so that you can begin to find answers that lead you to grow and change course OUT of the dilemma. To give you new options for navigating the dilemma. The key component in all of these scenarios is to find the joy and gratitude for the whole of the journey that always has something of great value within it for us to find.

We came into this world with nothing, and we will leave this world with nothing as we have all heard many times before, I'm sure. The biggest part in between those two points in time, is our life! And what we do with that life! Do we accept the polarity principle that we cannot have sun without rain, north without south, the Yin and the Yang, the good and the bad etc.?

Where on your timetable is gratitude? Is it prominent throughout your day not just when life is good, but when times are hard? And when life seems most difficult and unbearable, can you still find joy amidst the chaos? To find your way through the storms of life, gratitude and joy must be your constant companions.

Let me repeat that: to find your way through the storms of life, gratitude and joy must be your CONSTANT companions.

Remember that our creator's thoughts and ways are higher than ours as mere humans. He is there for us to connect to during all of life's happenings. He wants us to connect to Him to praise Him in the sunlight and in the darkness of the storm because He always knows the way through for our highest good!

He does not have to make his sun shine on this planet or create the constant seasons for our benefit, or hold the earth on its axis 24/7 as it spins perfectly each day around the sun for 365 days a year. He doesn't have to give us the glorious palette of colours in a sunrise or sunset. Neither does he have to give us animal life for our enjoyment, nature for nurturing our very being. His blessings upon us are infinite, they never cease!

So, will you sing the song of the sunflower each day? Will you shine your light like a beacon day in and day out no matter what is before you? Will you master mindfulness and live gratefully in each present moment?

The past is gone, it cannot affect us in the present moment, the only moment where the magic of life unfolds. The future is an illusion because it hasn't happened yet, so why worry over it?

An ancient sage of great wisdom 3,000 years ago, Lao Tsu tells us that *"the greatest gift we can give to the world, is that of our own transformation"* that is; to relinquish all the darkness within our soul and shine with the goodness and light from above.

So, when you find yourself sinking or heavily burdened, raise your eyes above, think of your face as that of a sunflower seeking the warmth and healing of the sun's rays; and ask yourself: "What would love do next?" And do that!

For me, love expresses gratitude and joy for every part of my journey … consistently in all the weathers of my life!

~ 19 ~

For life is about loving, living, laughing, singing, sharing and learning to dance in the rain as well!!

Namaste.

Mandy E. Robinson

Two-Time Canadian Provincial Award Recipient:

2015 Provincial Award, Ontario Canada,

Leading Women Building Communities recognition program.

Canadian Provincial Volunteer Award Recipient – Multiple Sclerosis Society.

In 2015 crowned the first female Ambassadorial Town Crier for Cobourg, Ontario Canada.

An accomplished professional speech writer for all occasions, Mandy is the recipient of the:

Prestigious Distinguished Toastmaster Award.

8 Times Best Selling Author.

Professional Published poet:

Creating Custom Poems for all events and ceremonies.

Professional Published Photographer: Front Cover Featured Photo for Canadian National Magazine – *More About Our Canada*

Triple MMM Coaching - Women's Empowerment Coach.

Legacy Ghostwriter, Editor, Proofreader, *Illumination One Page* for website, blog, story - all options customized to your preference.

Among her professional endeavours, she also has extensive experience as a Spokesperson, Inspirational Keynote Speaker, Visual Storyteller, Recap Specialist, TV Show Host/Creator, TV Show Co-Host, Events MC, Town Crier for All Events.

Mother of 3 girls and one son who left this world far too soon.

Grandmother of an incredible, beautiful-hearted grandson of 14 years.

Contact information:

Email: freedm49@gmail.com

Email: cobourgtowncrier@gmail.com

https://www.facebook.com/mandy.robinson.376

LinkedIn: /in/mandy.robinson-1b632647

Phone: 905-396-5351

Chapter 3

SURVIVING

Leigh Renaud

Have you ever taken the time to really look at a Sunflower field in the wind, each sunflower blowing in its own direction, some standing taller than the others, while others sort of fade away in the distance, it's the most remarkable thing, I've ever seen.

Sunflowers have always been fun character flowers for me, I love how when you walk through a field, they all seem to lift their heads up to greet you like you've been best friends for years. They are such a welcoming flower.

Every Sunflower petal blazing in yellow, soaked in infinite possibilities, new friendships, and new beginnings. A grounded stem, thick, bound deep in the earth, spreading its roots and learning to grow.

I am Leigh, I am a survivor of child abuse, sexual child abuse, rape, domestic violence, assault, and attempted murder. I also survived two toxic marriages, my oldest daughter's car accident that almost took her life and my 24-year-old daughter's, suicide. I have seen pain, that no person should endure. I continue to go to therapy, I thrive as a positive mature career woman who opened her own business, in spiritual awareness, guidance and relationship alignment.

I won't blow sunflower dust at you, it takes infinite awareness of who you are to "SURVIVE," so much sadness and violence. I may never be healed, but I will always strive to be the best version of myself. I have learned to simply accept that I come with "Triggers." I spent a long time designing a package that helped me identify "My Triggers," and I continue to use it daily. It's a way for me to track my emotions and keep me on a manageable routine. In crisis, all I had to fall back on was routine. It helped me structure the focus I needed to be able to survive the pain.

Not all prisons come as a small desolate grey room with concrete walls and floors. My prison was a 5500 sq. foot home with lavish fixings, hardwood floors and gardens. No matter how many people resided in our prison, my husband made it a place of fear and discontent. The first thing I burned when he left was a wooden board sign that read, *Our Love Story Starts Here*. This was anything but a "Love Story."

Looking back there were so many faked holidays, he hated holidays and made sure no one enjoyed one. It wasn't always like this, there were moments of decency and kindness, but they just became fewer and fewer until there were none.

We met in a hospital room, he was the brother of a family friend, the night we met my short-term boyfriend had hurt me badly. I was late picking him up in his car, he was drunk and angry. He took the car from me angrily and drove erratically. When I asked to get out, he let me, he dragged me out by my hair and then proceeded to punch me in the face several times. Angels were watching me that night. I was rescued abruptly by a police officer and her husband on their way home from a Christmas party. They drove me home, called the police and had my future husband drive me to the hospital.

There was a moment in the hustle of the busy emergency room when he wiped away the dry blood from my bruised and swollen face, when I fell in love with his kindness. He made me smile during a time of complete darkness. Through his compassion that night, that's the man I fell in love with. That's how my fairytale marriage began. I remember going home after, standing in the shower washing the rest of the blood and dry mud off my tiny, battered body and thinking, new beginnings are here. He told me that night he couldn't believe a man could treat a woman so badly. What else would a monster say?

Our first three years together we magical, that's why the first time he hit me I was so easy to forgive. Thinking back, the moments when he would hit me were the easy times. It is the emotional and financial abuse that haunts me today.

I spend every day wondering when he will return to finish the job and end my life. So, I live in fear, I work in fear, terrified to leave my own home. There weren't enough cameras, bars, or alarm systems to make me feel secure again, our ongoing court case continues.

I am unable to date or be near a man, it seems so far away. I am learning to trust people slowly. My healing started with victim services. They gave me ten sessions of therapy for free and then, back to the world, back to your life, back to your job, and your kids! I couldn't get past it. It started affecting my everyday life, I couldn't stop picturing him taunting me.

My marriage ended differently than most, it became an NBC movie. After finding out about his ongoing affairs with several women, I ended things. He wouldn't let it go. He would later sneak into our room and have sex with me while I was half sedated, in the home where my children lay sleeping above me. This happened twice. The first time was so bad I found myself back in that well-lit hospital room. He drove me there; he didn't dare come with me. He picked me up, and for a few days he was kind and within a few weeks, I experienced a very similar situation. Only this time he instilled more fear, pressed his lips against my ear, and made sure I knew he was never leaving.

"You are never leaving me, Leighanna." I still wake up to the sound of his voice.

The next day I asked him to leave. Instead, I was given 30 minutes to take a few things and he threw me up the stairs to go be with my family. My disabled daughter and her children, her oldest son 12, and newborn twin boys, lived upstairs. He also removed my granddaughter who was 13 at the time, I had just gotten custody of her, ten months before. I wasn't allowed access to my home, or my things. He blocked off our doorway so I couldn't have access.

This went on for weeks, he had moved another woman into my home. She slept in my bed, ate off my dishes, interacted with my pets. I found out about her on Cats of Instagram, she posted her love for the cat he bought me for my birthday, a Scottish Fold named, Solomon. It was hash tagged, "They Love Me Already." A part of me was relieved he was someone else's problem. I was grateful he was no longer part of my life.

It was November, I grew tired of not having my things. I texted him several times but he was nonresponsive. I decided to be brave that day and break into our part of the house and get my stuff. I was driven, I was getting my things, I just wanted to wear my own underwear. It seemed perfectly rational; he moved on, yet he dangled my personal belongings like trophies, making me beg for every scrap of what I owned.

I knocked on that door 40 times or more. No answer. Then I

kicked it open. Only, he was there, with her. She wore my robe proudly; he immediately became violent. He hurt me, he hurt my disabled daughter, several times. Our 20-minute interaction became more and more volatile. He managed to catch the last five minutes on video where I threw a Buddha head at her. It bounced off the couch and hit her leg. Let me explain. My body was bruised again by his hand. I looked over and saw her laughing, while he hit me and something dark inside me finally snapped. The way she smiled and laughed it was sickest thing I have ever witnessed. The police came, they spent their time with him, I found myself removed from my home and in a prison cell. No one asked me a single question, no one cared. Not one person cared about what happened to me. My daughter and mother begged them to just listen to my story.

I live with the desperate cries of my 78-year-old blind mother, crying and screaming that she will find a way to get me out. I spoke very little during the drive there. I was vibrating with fear. I was 50 years old; I had never been arrested. I had never felt this type of fear.

My oldest son and his wife came and signed me out several hours, later. I wasn't allowed on my property. I stayed with my sister, while he tortured my family, daily. He would sneak around my daughter's space at night, steal from her, while daily torturing her family and her new babies, by placing speakers in the ceiling and turning the music up to insane volumes. The police did nothing to help. That was the power he held at his man's club, that's the power he still has.

He was later charged with a multitude of crimes.

We are currently in court.

He continues to battle with my daughter for a house she bought after the car accident that almost killed her. She trusted her stepfather of 18 years to be on the mortgage. He paid nothing in the two years he was there, threatening to take her house every day he was there. We all tried so hard to make it work. He immediately filed a petition to make her sell her house. He has already taken so much from this family.

We are currently still fighting this battle as well, struggling through lawyers, and insanely high lawyer bills.

I am currently on medical leave at work, my mental health was greatly affected by the events I survived.

As a family, we pull together, we make the most of every day. I started a small business a few years back part-time after my regular job. I still live in fear most days. My home business gave me a safe haven. After all I had seen, and survived, there wasn't a moment for a long time where I didn't feel like I wanted to die. I still often sit in grief and self-hatred for allowing this awful human to come into our lives. They tell me it's survivors' guilt, PTSD. My fear, this fear has been lonely. Few can understand what it's like to marry a monster, I thought.

My intuitive Tarot business guided me to so many women, so many similar stories and for the first time I realized I was not alone. Sadly, I can tell with confidence that one out of every three women will experience abuse by the time they are 18. These are from the statistics of women who report. Just imagine if we all did.

The most important man in my life these days is God. My spirituality grew so strong after what happened to me. I opened

The Tipsy Gypsy 2.0 in 2021, I started a very interactive TikTok channel. I started by reading Tarot cards, I was always good at that and it's so different than being an account manager, it became a nice balance. I spend my evenings on TikTok live or doing collective readings, I have now branched out with private sessions.

I have really enjoyed this part of my life. I know I can't focus on full-time work still; so, this has been an incredible experience. I have met some of the most important people in my life. I continue to heal and grow every day, knowing that God will always guide me to the next amazing adventure.

Although a lot of things still need time to heal, open court cases will one day be closed and I know no matter what I have an amazing family, together, we will pull through. One day we will all be on the shores of a beach, vaguely reminded of the time, I married a monster.

Leigh Renaud

Leigh grew up in Etobicoke, ON. She is a seasoned Sales Manager with over 20 years of experience. Leigh is currently an Account Sales Manager with a telecommunications company. She also developed her own business recently - *The Tipsy Gypsy 2.0.*

She is an intuitive Tarot Reader and content creator on TikTok, Instagram, Facebook, and YouTube. Leigh has developed her own content for over a year now and has a very successful following. She is becoming widely known for her work with Recovery Rituals, a segment she designed and created herself during her personal trauma.

Leigh is a mother of three, Amanda, Andrew, and Jensen; a grandmother of eight, Mackenzie, Zayden, Madison, Owen, Dante,

Damien, Isla and Reese. While Leigh is a professional career woman, you can find her cooking and baking up a storm, with her family. Leigh also enjoys yoga, dancing, and spending evenings in front of the fireplace watching a great murder mystery.

To contact Leigh:

TikTok : The Tipsy gypsy 2.0

www.thhetipsygypsy2.shop

1 705 305-1757

leighannakramshoj@gmail.com

Chapter 4

CONQUERING STRUGGLES

Rob White

I write this story in the hopes that it can inspire someone by sharing some personal struggles I've overcome in my life. It's real, it's raw and authentic. Whether you agree with some of what I did or opinions I may have on some subjects, I cannot change the past. The only thing I know, for sure is that I know nothing.

Growing up in a blue-collar family I would say I had a pretty amazing time for most of my childhood. I always enjoyed being outside, capturing creatures, like frogs and toads, insects, and snakes. So much so, that my grade 8 librarian bought me a huge book on entomology. Based on the books I used to check out, in short, I was very different than most other kids.

I know that my love for professional wrestling always made me stand out in my grade 8 year. This was horrible though, as my two best friends turned on me that year, making it a miserable experience for me, so I did not attend my Grade 8 graduation. I never explained why to anyone They said they were going to take LSD and shoot me when I got into grade 9. I was a complete loner and really had no friends.

I remember how intimidating it was in that new environment, only made worse by my math teacher being a really intimidating figure. I always struggled with math. He would call you up to the blackboard and totally rip you apart if you could not solve the problem. Saying things like, "Has the gel in your hair seeped into your brain and made you stupid?" in a booming voice in front of the whole class.

It was devastating to my confidence. I had to attend summer school to pass grade 9. On my exam, I didn't answer any questions. I just berated him for how he had treated me. Fast forward to grade 10, and I started to make friends, ironically with a group from my public school whom I had never been friends with. These were some of my first experiences — smoking marijuana and feeling like I belonged again.

I walked in being a mix of defensive, angry and cut off from the world sort of a person. I would scream at anyone who crossed my path, particularly the hospital staff. I was sick of the wrongs of the world. I could be heard through the halls of the hospital screaming about how I was fed up with these crimes and ranting about how I was sick of it all.

I was saying things like, "You think I don't know what is going on here?" I had my shirt off and was directing my anger at any of the staff who got near me, while my father was trying to calm me down a couple of feet away. By this time, there were at least thirty hospital staff surrounding me; I was encircled by them.

Something had told me to take off all my clothes and the answer to cure all diseases was in my blood. I would say this scene lasted about 18-25 minutes with none of the staff entering my proximity. I was in a fit of rage and it was quite intimidating to anyone witnessing this episode.

I started to undo my pants when a familiar face approached me with tears in his eyes. He then asked me, "What is wrong?" I had known this man from high school; he was a short man with a baby face. It was a man named Kirk. Although I didn't know Kirk very well, he used to buy weed back in high school.

To this day I'm not sure if it was the tears in his eyes or the look of genuine concern, but it triggered something inside me and I broke. I believe I said, "Nick" as everyone around me was masked up. This man put his hands on my shoulders and snapped me out of the rage.

I then collapsed to my knees and was surrounded by hospital staff. I cried out to God and the staff made their move and secured me. I recall asking the staff if they were going to do this to me again. They strapped me to a bed. I truly believed they were going to crucify me as I felt they were part of the satanic medical system to make sure I would not return to earth.

I will never forget that Halloween when my friend Travis had purple weed and we smoked it. We then went to his house, and I had the biggest laughter fit of my life. I was trying to eat cake. We couldn't look at one another without bursting out laughing. You just had to be there.

Shortly after, I contracted mononucleosis and was soon hospitalized, given penicillin and almost passed away. It was then I realized that I was allergic to it. I failed the whole year as I was bedridden for months and slept all the time away. I made a strong comeback in grade 11 as I was told that I would have to redo grade 10 otherwise.

I had heard that you could make friends with the stoner community easily. Somehow, I became the guy that everyone needed to get weed from. I had the right connections to the point that my dealer was sick of me coming over all the time.

I made the decision I was going to run marijuana for him and he agreed that he would lend me the product on the spot. This dealer would then decide what monetary amount I was to pay and that's when things got really bad socially for me. I became well-known and extremely popular.

I took on a part-time job at a local restaurant as a dishwasher. I became the guy who sold weed to everyone, my manager, my co-workers, and my peers. It was common to hear, "Rob you're the man." Of course, I knew many of these friends were artificial, but it still felt very rewarding.

At the time, my father offered me a job doing residential garbage disposal for my summer break. That job sure showed me what I was capable of physically, as it was a brutal job that required me to lift 30 lb. bags of garbage by myself in extreme weather conditions. It challenged me physically and nothing was better than coming home and smoking my bongs in the basement.

People would often stop over and continued to purchase their pot from me. I did not know the risks that lay ahead. This would be the introduction to the rave scene for me. I'll never forget being invited to my first rave and being afraid to go out. A pill was put in my hand and against my better judgement, I took the pill and had the time of my life.

I was involved in the rave scene for about a year. For one year of my life, 52 weeks in a year, I went to 34 parties total, where I engaged in risky behaviours, such as drug use on the weekends. The scene changed and I stopped going.

School had finished and I started working full-time throwing garbage. I was still engaged in selling weed, however, I was saving money. I knew from the very young age of 21 the difference between needs and wants.

I had about $100,000 saved up. I started experiencing pain in the lower left side of my back. This was Sciatica nerve issues; thankfully the contract came to an end, and I was lucky to be able to take roughly three months of work off.

I realized that I had to let my body heal and knew I was about to experience some changes that I did not see coming. I would go through a devastating breakup with my high-school sweetheart. When in a relationship, I tend to love really hard. This was my entire world at the time.

My instincts are above and beyond average and I felt that something was off, as she told me she was going to have a lady's night out. I decided to take a stroll down Main Street and walked by the bar to see her sitting on top of an Orlando Bloom-looking man.

That was the start of the end of us and it took everything out of me not to start crying, even at work. I will always be grateful to her for listening to me and sharing stories of hardships as she always helped me through painful times. She was the first girl I ever asked to marry me and that had helped save me.

In the process of taking time off from working, I found peace in having various friends come over to play video games or watch wrestling, as I was trying to figure out my next move in life. Never being much of a drinker, a couple of my friends started bringing beers over regularly. This happened more frequently, and it soon become more of an activity than it ever had before.

My friend Alex and I would hang out a lot, and he was one of the only friends that I could really challenge when it came to video games. With Alex, I could discuss imaginative ideas when it came to the nature of reality, and its consciousness, the mysteries of the universe and conspiracy theories. I remember it was a windy night, when it happened. We were doing our usual activities when my mind started going into some pretty strange thoughts.

My father worked for this company BFI, I started to think and actually believe that it was just a cover story for him working for the FBI. My mind was fixated on some pretty outlandish ideas about who I was. A lot of this was fueled by a feeling I had since I was a teen. This feeling was of being special or important and meant for something greater in this world.

As the days went on, my mother began telling me that I had to go to the hospital, and that something was wrong. I just didn't seem to understand why I was being told this. During this time, I do recall exhibiting some strange behaviours. There was a Saturday night when my father was listening to music in the living room. I had grabbed my rave shirt and came upstairs to play his favourite Elvis songs. My mind began to tell me I was Elvis reincarnated. I believed this so much so, that I told my parents that.

I can only imagine what they must have been thinking. During this stage of my life, there were a lot of side stares because of some of the beliefs I had. This time of my life is still a blur, some of the more prominent events I have memories of. Eventually, my father convinced me to go to the hospital. I was then placed on a 72-hour psychiatric watch so I could be assessed to figure out what was happening to me, although I still believed I was fine.

I cannot recall how often I was in and out of the hospital as my memories are not in chronological order. I do remember having many strange thoughts and my mother telling me after bloodwork had been received there was an astronomical amount of THC in my system. I was later diagnosed with Bipolar disorder which I still did not believe. I was encouraged to take medications. I didn't want to take these medications and felt everyone around me was pushing me to take them. Many tried to normalize these medications and there were many visits to the psychiatry ward at the hospital.

I found these visits quite pleasant, and it was a local hospital and I received regular treatment. Things settled down after that. I have no idea what pills or injections they were giving me at the time. Now, one thing to know during this time was, that it was not as if I would just come right out and say to people that I was Jesus, it's that I believed everyone knew who I was, and it was a big secret being kept in Canada until the world was ready for my arrival.

It's tough to remember the exact chain of events looking back at this now. It exists only in memories that I have to try to put them in order. When I talk about it, then it flows; but writing about it is a little more challenging than I expected. There are so many little stories and memories from events at that time of beautiful connections I made with other patients.

There are also the talks I had with psychiatrists, struggling to understand what was going on in the longest hospital visits. I was sent by ambulance from Newmarket.to Penetanguishene to stay at their facility for three weeks. This is where I believe I finally began to come out of my delusional Psychotic break, or spiritual attack,

so many things I labelled it. The facility was nice - more of a comfy dorm room atmosphere, as opposed to the jail-like one that Newmarket had become.

Deep down, I was beginning to come to the most logical explanation of what had happened to me. I was starting to believe that my lifestyle had caught up with me — too much pot, smoking, experimenting with too many different substances in the rave scene, lack of sleep and finally adding alcohol when I was trying to let my back heal.

I was the social butterfly of that facility. I was the most outgoing guy there. I was happy and enthusiastic. I did have some profound experiences there that are hard for me to explain to anyone, as I am the only one who knows they happened, and they were very real.

Finally, after three weeks of observation, at my meeting with the top psychiatrist psychologist, Kim, we talked for a while. To my relief, I remember him saying, the words, "We can't find anything wrong with you, Robert, take better care of yourself." I was relieved to be told I could go home.

I'm not sure that was the best thing for me, though new rules were set for me at home, like no smoking pot. I spent enough time being an inpatient at the hospital so they could check up on me and give me the tools to move forward. All it would involve would be monitoring my blood, as by that time I was prescribed lithium and Zyprexa, a little yellow pill that I took before bed that dissolved in my mouth and tasted like an M&M.

Ironically, when you woke up, it felt exactly like being really, stoned on marijuana. I was not a fan of taking those medications. The lithium caused me, in a span of about three months, to go from

180 pounds to about 250 pounds. That, combined with the fact that

all my friends had seemed to disappear, I fell into the deepest depression I've ever known struggling with trying to understand what happened to me and watching everyone else move on with their lives like I never existed.

I stopped caring about my appearance and let my beard grow. I just didn't care anymore. I recall talking to my psychiatrist at the time, and told him I was done with his medication and that I was not going to be taking it anymore. His exact words were, "You'll never amount to anything without the medication". I proceeded to tell him, "You don't care about me at all, and your only solution to anything is pushing pharmaceuticals on me so you can get your kickbacks from the drug companies."

I never went back to see him again. Feeling lost and alone, I went to see my family doctor. I broke down and cried in his office. He didn't handle it well, it seemed to make him very uncomfortable. He convinced me to try an antidepressant called Effexor. I tried it, and I remember, listening to my brain, sizzling and popping in my head. It was horrible. I just wanted it to stop. I had tried a lot of stuff in my day, but nothing like that. I could literally hear my brain sizzling and popping. I stopped taking it immediately.

Being lost, and alone, and not having anyone to turn to, I fell back into my old routine of self-medicating. Only two of my former friends or acquaintances ever made an effort to help me. My younger friend, Mark, used to look up to me, would stop by and try and get me to come out and get out of my rut. My friend, Anthony, came over a few times to be there and listen. He often gave me the most direct and profound advice as he had a way of

putting things so simply that it could solve your issue in a sentence and it just made sense during this time.

I was exposed to cocaine by a member of the Hell's Angels. I found something to look forward to at that time and chasing that high was it. In the span of three months, I spent $10,000 on that crap. I didn't care if I lived or died at the time. I just wanted to see the pain stop, and it did the trick.. Over the course of time, all that money I had saved for my future dwindled to nothing. I was lost, alone, and really had no one to rely on other than Mark and Anthony.

There are only so many times you can be told the same things and I felt like a burden to them. After a while, I can't say where it came from, but one day I woke up and said, "Enough." Something deep inside me knew it was now or never and I could not go on living like that. I stopped the cocaine use overnight, got off my overweight butt and decided I was going to go back into the garbage industry.

This time if I wanted a future in it. I would need to get my DZ license. Having literally no money left, and no car, there was only one solution. I had to hit the pavement and look for a job to be able to get a car again. I could save up money for truck driving school to secure that license. I found a factory about a 30-minute walk from my home and got hired on as a temp employee where I would plug cell phones in and load some kind of program on them.

The factory fixed and repaired electronics of all kinds. I was happy in that little role for a while until the loading phone program was done. I was moved from integrated media into another sector doing certain checks on phones and printing labels

for the most part of that job. I hated every minute of it. I felt like a lifeless drone surrounded by people who actually seemed like they knew what they were doing.

Oftentimes, when I would run out of work, I would take one of the phones, go to the bathroom and play games. Nobody ever seemed to know, but I know I was gone for long periods of time. I made some friends there, of course, but the most frustrating part was being trained on other things I did not want to do, by people who spoke terrible English. While trying to train you, there are only so many times you can say, "Sorry can you say that again?" before you just give up.

Just let me stay in my little spot and leave me alone. It was the most mind-numbing work I had ever done but I needed it to save the money, although most of my thoughts at the time were that I had to get out of there. Soon enough, that decision would be made for me as during a lunch break, I decided to smoke a joint, in an effort to just zone out as it was really taking its toll on me spiritually working there. I guess someone noticed and I was called into my manager's office and fired. She was really nice about it and said it's really too bad Rob and we really liked you here.

That did not compute with me, as I know I gave minimal effort, but perhaps my personality pulled me through as I did get along well with most people there. Feeling relieved that I would never have to go back to that job — ironically, I found a job right next door at U-Haul, where my friend was a salesman.

The U-Haul job lasted three to four months. It wasn't as bad as the factory, but I still did not like it much. I got fired for doing something wrong on one of the computers but was relieved again that I would not have to go back. I had finally saved up enough to

go for my truck license. I found Rogers School of Transport Training about a 40-minute bus ride north of me and I signed up for the course.

Upon completion of the course, I started to get my confidence back. It felt so good setting a goal and achieving it. I was beginning to get my groove back. Once I got that licence, now I needed a job.

I talked to the garbage truck driver. He was picking up at my house and I asked him about it. He told me they were always looking for guys and where to go to apply. I went down to the yard at Turtle Island Recycling and had a chat with the supervisor there. He told me that I would need to start at a temp agency and where to go for that.

I was pretty excited and I made some pretty bold claims to that supervisor. I told him I was going to be the number one guy there as I knew that I was capable of in the line of work from my previous experience. I told them for the first three months that I did not want to drive the trucks but only load them to get back into shape for the job and that's exactly what I did.

I had a fire burning inside me as I knew this was it. This is what I was going to do, and I was going to be the best at it. Quite frankly, I came in there like a maniac and outperformed everyone that was working there. My life literally depended on it. Within a year, I went from being a temp making $15 an hour to becoming the lead hand of the town making $22 an hour.

Every morning for three years, I came to work super excited as I felt. I got my life back on track and I literally worked as fast and as hard as I could to make the biggest impression I could, but also because I genuinely enjoyed doing the work as it was quite the adrenaline kit working as hard as I was.

I found myself a girlfriend who worked at a Mercedes dealership, and we moved in together in a basement apartment. That didn't last as she moved out after two years and the place was all mine, with my rent being $800 a month. I tapped into the old me and saved my money like no tomorrow, as the goal was to buy a house. After eight years of working, I was able to save $250,000 to make that happen. I'm currently on my 17th year there, where I have had no accidents or tickets which is extremely rare in that industry.

A lot has happened during that time — I could write a whole book about my work experience there. You wouldn't believe the stories I could tell. I had lost touch with my roots in nature, but having a daughter now has re-awakened that aspect of my soul. I still enjoy going out into nature and discovering the amazing magical creatures that exist all around us.

Reflecting on all of this, I cannot necessarily say, I'm proud of that past and what I did in my younger years, but I can tell you, that I wouldn't change it.

I always found growing up that society always said, don't do drugs, but push them in the music and movies, as if it was the cool thing to do. What I am proud of is pulling myself out of that dark cloud, or an abyss that I fell into. I easily could have bought their diagnosis and collected disability for the rest of my life, but I knew I was better.

I was never bipolar I had just lived fast and hard and my mind had some kind of psychotic break. Needless to say, I became somebody again through hard work and determination. I overcame that alternate reality so easily. Over my years of working in the garbage and recycling industry, I have worked with, and trained many guys from all over the world. I have helped lots of

young men who have come across as being lost in life by relating that story of what I overcame.

I try to give them good advice about the difference between

~ 43 ~

needs and wants and how to get ahead. I've always been a pretty lucky guy. When I was a really young kid, I would wander the neighbourhood, looking into my neighbour's window wells, the two- foot deep metal enclosures that were by people's basement windows. I would find that toads would jump into them and never get out so I would go around looking at them to get the toads out of there. I've often wondered if that bought me a lot of good karma points that I redeemed later on in my life.

I'll never know why all those events happened to me or what it really meant. Why did I ever believe I was Jesus Christ? I did not grow up in a family that seemed to believe it, or that went to church. What I can tell you was that it was truly a profound experience and I felt incredibly powerful during that time.

What does it all mean? Why me? Everyone else around me seemed to be doing the same things at that time. Sometimes I wonder if it was a spiritual attack and other times I think, well perhaps my brain just could not keep up with the lifestyle I was living. Maybe I had a kundalini awakening and reached Christ consciousness, and did not know how to handle it at my level of perception.

At that time, there were incredible experiences only I knew had happened and that were true. Maybe no one more than me needed to hear the story again, to propel myself in my life these days. If I could go back and do it all again, I would have stayed away from all that stuff. I would've tried to pursue my dream of becoming a professional wrestler as I believe I would have had

what it took to achieve that based on how hard I was able to push myself during my working career.

I was once a radiant sunflower that shone brightly in the fields.

I reached for the sky and above. Many in the field weathered a severe storm like the one that humbled me and snapped me in half and brought me down to the dirt.

At some point, I chose to rise again and not give up. I'm proud of being able to overcome, not collapse in my life. It was by far the greatest personal struggle I have ever experienced in my 44 years.

I refused to participate in that system, because I knew I didn't belong in it. To you the reader, I hope you can take something from my story. We all have struggles in our life and it seems like it's never going to get better. There is a lot of beauty in this wicked world, and we all have a choice to reach for that light and rise again even if we are only going to fall again.

Never give up. I had so much potential when I was younger. If only I had mentors. With mentors and guidance who knows what I would've been capable of. Surround yourself with positive, uplifting, people that inspire you. Seek mentors if you don't have the strive to push yourself through any darkness, you may be going through and never stop growing.

Do you shine your light on others if they need it and be proud of anything you have struggled through and overcome, no matter how small or insignificant it may seem? There are always others who can relate. Don't be afraid to share your story. Ask for help if you need it, learn to reprogram your subconscious mind and reach for the sky like a sunflower.

Rob White

Rob grew up in Brampton, Thorold and Richmond Hill, Ontario before settling in Newmarket in grade 4, where he graduated high school. He attended Rogers School of Transport Training to acquire a DZ license to operate garbage and recycling trucks and has now been doing so accident- and ticket-free for 17 years.

Never having much interest in sports, he was always drawn to professional wrestling and attended a professional wrestling school in his 20s which ultimately did not transition into a career as he had wished. His other primary interests are insects, reptiles, and amphibians. He spends time in the spring, summer and fall discovering said creatures while sharing his knowledge and experiences with his daughter to show her how we are surrounded by magical creatures if you know where to look.

Another major theme of his life was searching for truth in this world and questioning official narratives of what is taught in the mainstream. Rob has always been fascinated by ancient civilizations, such as Egyptian and Sumerian and ancient unexplained megalithic structures that suggest evidence of an ancient world-wide advanced civilization.

Recently he has discovered an interest in photography and is enjoying the town of Aurora where he currently lives while trying to achieve the dream of owning property in northern Ontario where he would like to live as self-sufficiently as possible while pursuing an Interest in learning about the edible and medicinal plants that grow in Canada.

Rob white 1 905 503 2629

Soitbeginsagain77@gmail.com

Chapter 5

Overcoming Carried Generational Pain

Nicole Bylow

1.   Memories

My dad was super good at Jeopardy because he spent so much time in jail, he would come and go out of our lives. He was first Nations and when he didn't live with us, he was either in jail or on the street. He always seemed happy when we would go to visit in jail, you could hear him making jokes with the guards all the way until he got to the waiting room, his booming voice and laugh echoing throughout the hollow walls of his concrete confines.

He didn't fit anywhere, my dad was misunderstood, it was hard for him to keep a job, and it had nothing to do with being lazy, he was a very hard worker. I think the main reason was his appearance, he wasn't necessarily tall, probably 6 feet, but he had broad shoulders and was burly, and he had a really deep voice.

When I was younger, for a few years, when we lived in a northern community of Ontario near Algonquin Park, there was very little cultural diversity and a lot of stereotyping (or fear). He was a Master Carpenter, but no one would hire him up there, small villages, small minds, I like to say.

I remember him when I was younger. He used to take me out and show me the rabbit trails, show me how to set a snare, point out the different animal prints and the animals we could spot. I would have been about four or five. My dad would seldom wear shoes or a shirt in the warm weather. His favourite things were fishing, and cooking. He took calligraphy in high school and had the most beautiful penmanship; he would write me letters from jail. I still have them, they were so precise and neat, it is strange how you can admire someone's ability to write neatly.

My own penmanship is very messy, mostly because my mind moves so fast that I cannot get the words down quickly enough before I forget them. My Dad also used to make us clothing on the sewing machine. My mother told me he had worked in a factory sewing, so he was very talented at it.

One thing I noticed about him was that he seemed most comfortable when he was in the bush, his stride would change; he walked confidently among the trees, a place in the world where he could feel at peace, a place that made sense to the chaos of his mind and the world he managed to survive in.

I remember chasing after a bull moose when he shot it on our property. I'm the one who found it first because I could run faster than him. Dad told me to run in the opposite direction to him, and then there it was, this giant crashing through the underbrush and crushing the small trees alongside me, I was so close to being trampled.

He told me to go toward the water at the river, that when they're dying, they just get very thirsty. It was my first last breath. I think that was the first animal I ever saw die. I love animals, it is something to see the light leave their eyes, being so young I just remember sitting beside it at the water's edge, it looked at me and then its spirit left, onto another journey somewhere else.

Now in my later years, my heart hurts when I lose an animal or see one left for the birds on the road.

My Dad always had the biggest personality in the room, always had a story or a joke to tell, my sister says she thinks it was his way of making people feel more comfortable around him and not fear him — like he had to play a part to make everyone else feel at ease.

I don't know if this was always the case, but I do remember he used to always make people laugh when he first met them; he liked to tease us kids and our friends. I speak about my Dad because I never got a chance to know him like I wanted to, he passed away at 53.

I was a complete mess for years after, and that is when I started on my journey of healing. We knew dad was going to pass — it was something I was partially prepared for (Who really is ever prepared?)

I had never lost anyone close to me. But my next loss was one that made me fall to my knees, and I just barely got back up. My 19-year-old nephew who I loved like my own, was murdered, alongside his father, two of my favourite people in the world. They were stabbed so many times that you couldn't even recognize them anymore.

I can't remember the couple of years after this, the umbrella of PTSD decided to protect me. I almost went back to my darkness, which I will touch on later in this chapter.

2. Flashbacks

I started to think about the conglomeration of life events that shape us into who we are, the situations we are born into, and the goals we choose to pursue (or not) on our life path. From a very young age, I used to think and write about death and darkness and I can't explain why I had those thoughts, the morbid visions, many of my paintings were dark and bloody.

I think now that all of the time I spent pondering death when I was younger, was the creator giving me a heads-up, building my spiritual side up, so that later on in life I was able to reflect and put the pieces together, so they made sense somehow.

Some of my paintings were beautiful and had the ability to change a thought process without even being able to explain what that process was or what changed. I like to say my beautiful artwork is abstract, I poured my heart into it, a way to express myself that one cannot put into words.

In school, I have been studying social services and we have discussed a lot about generational trauma. It is carried within people from all walks of life and trickles down through your blood like a virus. Sometimes you don't understand why you feel a specific way, react a way to a certain sound or situation, and then you learn about the past of your parents and your grandparents and great-grandparents, and something clicks and there it is, that feeling finally makes sense.

3. Fear

I was sitting in Ojibwe class, and the epiphany was so profound that I immediately started to cry. The teacher was talking to some of my classmates about being able to imagine being separated from your family and being taken to a place where you couldn't speak your own language and nothing was explained to you, everything was just torn away. As she was speaking, I thought about the confusion, and the fear. She spoke the words "never knowing love", "not getting hugs and comfort and praise", just doing your chores and what you are told.

When I had my son and held him he was the most beautiful thing, I could never imagine having my own child, although I had helped raise my nephew from a baby.

It wasn't long before the C.A.S came into my life when my boy was just starting to walk, they were called for a domestic dispute. There was no violence, just arguing, but I decided to call the police, and immediately the C.A.S was involved.

When they came a day or two later they said that my husband (at the time) and I were not to be alone with our son, they didn't take him away, but I was mortified, I immediately felt unfit, less than, like the worst mother, on top of dealing with the pressure of having a toddler, the stress and feeling of worthlessness that the worker instilled in me was gut-wrenching.

I think that is when it first set in, the fear of loving him too deeply, because if he was taken away, I wouldn't be able to cope, I carried this fear around for so long without the knowledge of it plaguing me.

In the crevices of my mind, the dread playing itself out in nightmares, always running from something, spinning in circles and crawling across cold pavement with no control over the direction my limbs were going, confused terrified, and trapped. I still wake up soaked and in sweat and begging for some kind of peace, even after years of healing and counselling, I feel like I have barely dusted the surface off a mountain of dry bile.

From the fear of losing my whole world, that something would happen to him, no wonder there was a shield I kept up, that I couldn't love him wholly and completely, that I shackled myself and held back.

It pierced its claws into my very soul, it's in my genetics. Trauma that happened hundreds of years prior, generations before I even existed, how could I possibly recognize it, but ever present, ever real in those moments and your instincts take over and the reality of the past is all of a sudden, your own ... Generational Trauma.

4.   Bloodlines

In my case I got it from both sides, my grandparents were in foster homes, my parents were in foster homes, uncles, aunts, siblings, you get the idea.

What does this mean, you may ask, what is the point of this story? When you are removed from your family you lose a bond, you lose a feeling of being part of something and I'm not trying to say that each time this happens is a horrific event for the person in many cases it is necessary to protect the children. I have heard so many horror stories about foster homes and tend to wonder if even half the cases of removal are necessary. We don't know all the impacts, but we know without a doubt, that each and every time, the repercussions are unimaginable, unpredictable, and sadly many times harmful.

Recently we have been discussing vicarious trauma, when someone tells you stories about their lives or lived experiences, or possibly even stories that someone else has told them and although you are not the one who experienced it, it traumatizes you. Being a highly empathetic person, I have felt the trauma of the people I love, I have the memories clearly burnt into my mind, and the fear still suffocates me and tortures my soul.

I finally understood some of the emotional battles that my loved ones dealt with after I lost my nephew, I had felt it firsthand.

These type of events can break the strongest of minds. They say in my classes that we need to practise robust self-care; for me being able to listen to others and walk beside them in their healing involves being able to feel that pain and work through it with them.

I am very aware that I will need to work on the boundaries in my mind around empathy, and self-care may be more work than the actual job of being a listener.

Recently I have started to accept something about myself it's not something I've overcame it's something that I have had to accept. I'm starting to embrace it because it is uniquely mine and I know many other people probably suffer from a very similar thing and that's my mental health.

5.   The mind

I first got diagnosed with depression when I was 12 and I never really knew how it came or why, but I just didn't want to feel I was angry or upset. I was sad, I was ambiguous about my own feelings, and it didn't help that I started to get bullied at school.

I never understood why I got bullied. This was something that I've continued to have to deal with through my whole entire life. It seems like they always pick on the most sensitive person in the class or the one who's genuinely going to be upset. It's like they know they want to just engorge and feast themselves on your suffering.

It wasn't until later on down the road that I realized that they too are suffering. And I had something that they didn't have and that was the ability to wear my suffering on my sleeve without anyone ever asking me to — like anyone would ask you to do that anyway but it's like I never had the ability to hide it, not until I grew harder.

You know you make yourself into that pearl, that diamond, that thing that can withstand some tremendous amount of heat. You are the thing that had to roll around a thousand times in turmoil and muck to finally become so hard to the world that there was nothing that could affect it or hurt it. Nothing that could take away or give to it.

That hardness that I developed became a very scary place, became part of me, but I never want to go back to it, I never want to see it again. I never want it to show its head again. I've learned that that hardness — that was what the world needed me to become, hateful, and passionless. I needed to know these emotions, so I could understand others better.

My fall from grace lasted a few years, that's what they wanted, the ones in control, they want that fear and the continuous spoiling of our soul, they need it to make a profit. It causes war, disease, and the literal desolation of one's soul, until people numb themselves with pharmaceuticals to just get through the day. The ones in control are greedy for money and nothing fulfills them, except the feeling of overpowering others and holding us under their thumb.

But I didn't let them have me, I learned that the hate in that darkness and that egotistical part that you develop to prevent hurt, to protect yourself is the worst thing that you could ever do. People are beaten down to the point that you just want to be able to control someone or something because maybe you never had any control.

In my case, I have learned that trying to fight an invisible enemy is always a losing battle. It takes time and patience to understand oneself, and most of all self-forgiveness. This life is not a straight and narrow road, there will be much quicksand and many potholes on the way.

When I finally did realize that I needed to be on mood stabilizers, I was so sensitive that I couldn't be logical, so big pharma did help in a way, but not to the point that I was a complete zombie. They diagnosed me with a couple of different things. I'm not really sure if they were correct but whoever really knows?

I know now that I need to be on mood stabilizers and I take them regularly. I finally realized I had ADHD in my 30s and asked to speak to a specialist. It's been a battle, to say the least, but I think I'm winning. I understand that not everyone is meant to function the same way and I function differently, finally being treated for ADHD, has helped me to focus a lot more and not feel completely exhausted because I had ten things, I wanted to accomplish that day and I only did about half of them.

Understanding my illness has helped me not to have as much self-loathing and more confidence in my ability to somehow make a difference in society. Maybe I can't fit in a specific niche, but I can fit in somewhere and be okay with who I am.

6. Creator

In the past two years, I have become very spiritual. I believe that the Creator loves all of us and we are all on a journey. We're all on a journey to become perfected so that we may leave this world with our souls purer than they arrived. Sometimes I talk to my family that is no longer here and I feel that they are out there in the universe and can hear me.

It gives me some kind of inner peace, my heart doesn't hurt quite as much knowing they are in the hands of someone or something that loves with its entirety and gives everything, just as our mother earth gives everything she has to offer.

Nicole Bylow

Nicole Bylow is 35 years old. She went to University at the age of 19 and got her Bachelor of Arts in English. It took her seven years for a three-year program and now she is currently studying at Georgian College to get her Bachelor of Arts in Social Work.

She grew up for the first six years of her life in Northern Ontario in a small village outside of Halliburton. She didn't know much of the world other than what was in the backyard. She later moved to Parry Sound and then at the age of ten, to Orillia. She spent the next ten years living in Orillia.

At the age of 12, she moved out and lived with her sister to help look after her nephew and niece. Later, she got her own apartment at the age of 15 and had to learn how to juggle a relationship, a job, and school. Her mother and two brothers decided to move hours away and she decided to stay.

Nicole tried her best to do what was right, but it was definitely a struggle. She was only in two serious relationships — the one lasted seven years and he was her high school sweetheart. She decided to leave that relationship when he started to do hard drugs and she did not want that in her life as she had seen what it had done to people.

Her next relationship lasted about six years. She ended up having his child and got married. It was a very tumultuous time as sometimes it's very hard to know how to be in a relationship that's functional when you've never seen one firsthand.

Nicole loves to read and write and to spend time in nature camping, paddling, hiking, and swimming. She is a very forgiving person and tries to help whenever she can although this has come back to bite her many times, but she still remains this way. She is loyal to her family and friends and thinks she is fairly easygoing. Sometimes she can feel particularly strong about certain subjects or choices people make, in which case she may be a little bit hard-headed and take a break from the people she loves.

Generally, time heals the matter. Nicole is not really sure what the future holds, she's more of a fly-by-the-seat-of-your-pants person, but she does plan on moving out of the city one day and hopes to have a small hobby farm. She would love to have a piece of land for a vegetable garden, maybe some chickens and a goat. This is her first publication, and she is pleased to share some of her story of resilience.

Nicolebylow@gmail.com

1 705 770 6996

CONCLUSION

Throughout the chapters, you have read of many different struggles. Struggle comes in all forms and the experience is different for all. Many of us go through life oblivious to tragedy until it happens to us. From mental illness to abuse, enclosed in these pages there is one commonality. The willingness of these sunflowers to keep growing tall and keep reaching for the light.

We often have no control over what happens to us, but we do have control over how we choose to respond. We can choose to heal rather than let elemental forces of life decimate who we are. Our life experiences can force us to grow and really have a look at our own development.

Vulnerability is not a weakness, but a sign that despite our environment and conditions we can grow. A sunflower always reaches for the light and no matter what plants seeds of hope for others. If we let our stories go on without inspiring others, it is lost knowledge. Power comes from growth that challenges our being to the core and forces us to become better versions of ourselves.

We must reframe the incidents of life and look at them as "Life has happened for us, not to us." We must not get stuck in the past because, like a sunflower, we will rise up for the light time after time. We must collectively spread light, love and beauty to the world around us. Some may not always see the beauty, but these stories are reminders that no matter what you face, you can overcome anything.

Power comes from our mindset and ability to adapt. Sometimes, we adapt to survive and sometimes we adapt for our own peace. The journey of growth and healing begins when we start to take accountability for our condition and environment meaning, we choose to pick our own peace rather than victimize ourselves and exhibit self-sabotaging behaviours and thoughts.

Like the sunflower, we all serve a unique purpose and finding our own purpose isn't always easy, but it's worth it. Believe in yourself, heal mindfully, and hold no regrets. Letting go of past experiences that cannot be changed is a crucial part of success. We cannot change the past but rather how we view it.

When you turn your eyes toward a sunflower, our hope is that you will cherish its beauty and be reminded of the adversity you overcame. Let it be a reminder to always reach for the light, growth, and beauty.

These authors have shown courage and like others, their vulnerability in hopes that their message resonates and brings forth a feeling of hope. In conclusion, the songs these sunflowers have sung let us know we are never alone, and healing can come if we choose to conquer the inner parts of ourselves that need to be freed from the shackles of our minds and limiting beliefs we hold on to in the name of self-preservation. It's perfectly okay to sit in the darkness for a little while but eventually, we must reach for that light and bloom.

You are not what happened to you, you're an intricate and unique being. The light you hold has the power to change the world and should be shared. Sunflowers lean on one another and grow together. This is an unforgettable measurement of resilience in the name of survival, which leads to growth. When one grows and blooms, we all grow. And always reach for the light.

www.ingramcontent.com/pod-product-compliance
Lightning Source LLC
Chambersburg PA
CBHW071218120626
46546CB00006B/2618